Das wunderbare alte Ägypten

MALBUCH

☥

Malen Sie die erstaunlichsten
Designs der Wunder Ägyptens aus

Ancient World Editions

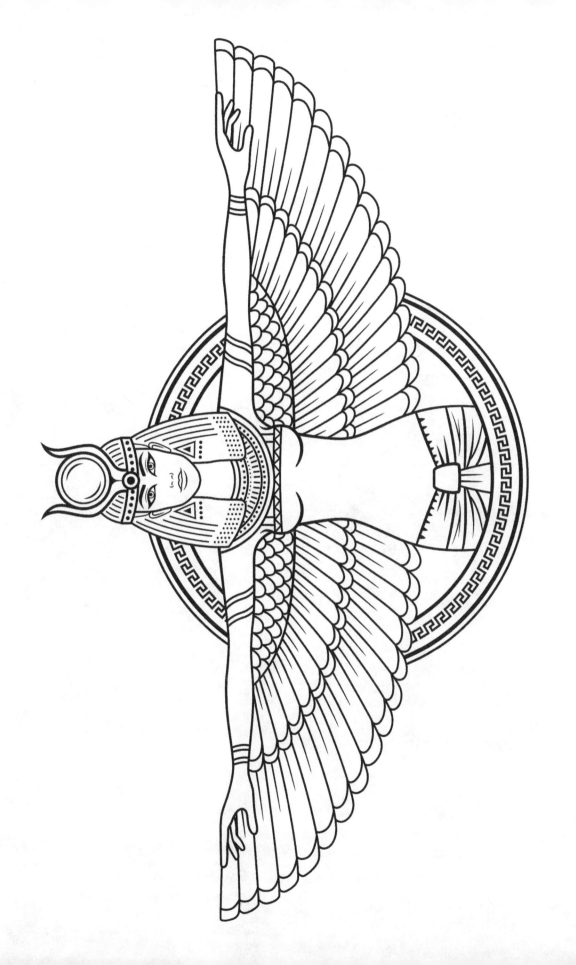

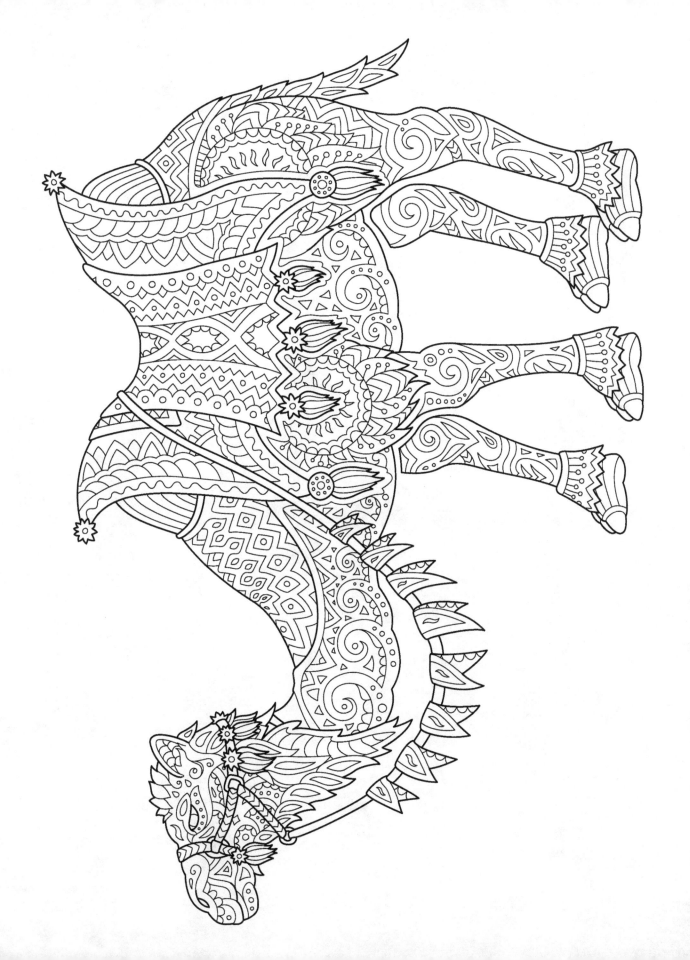

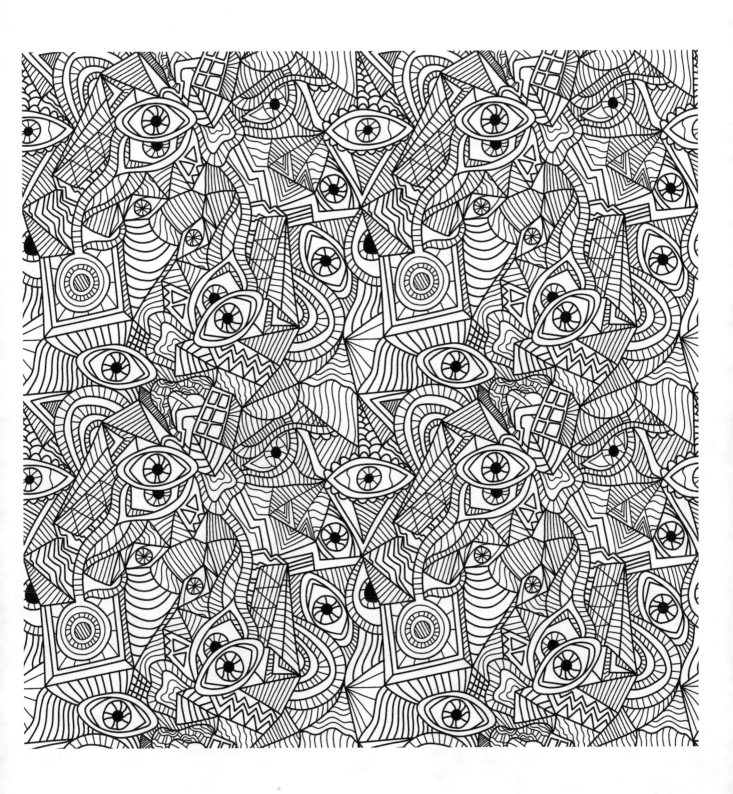

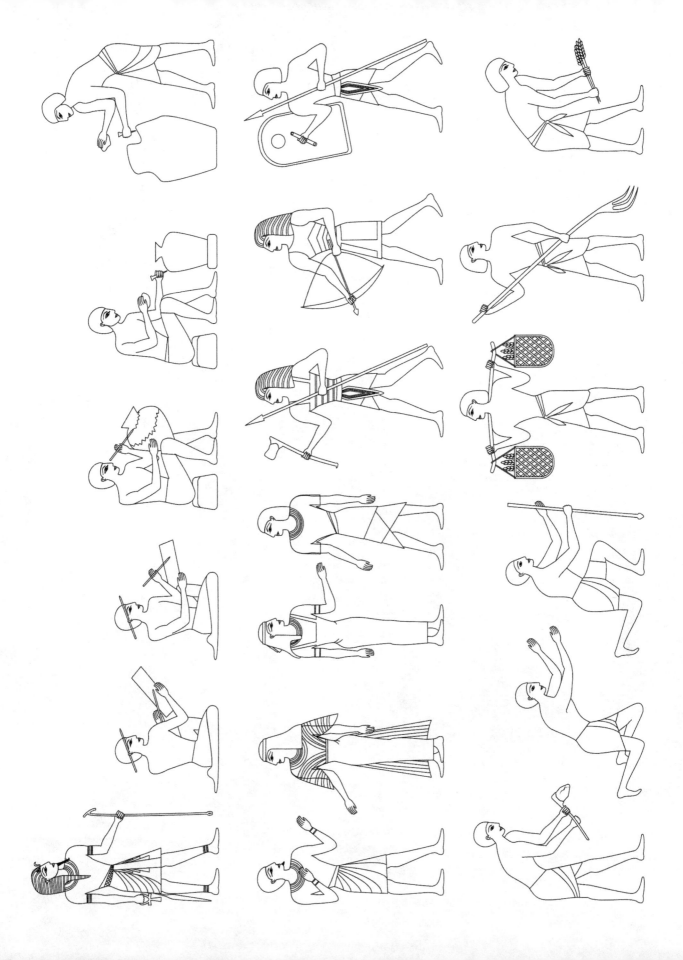

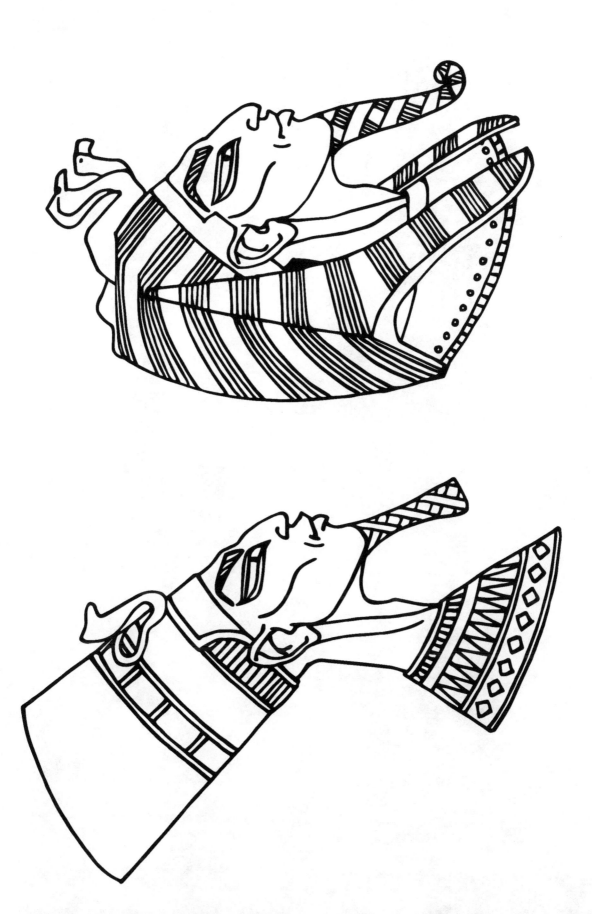

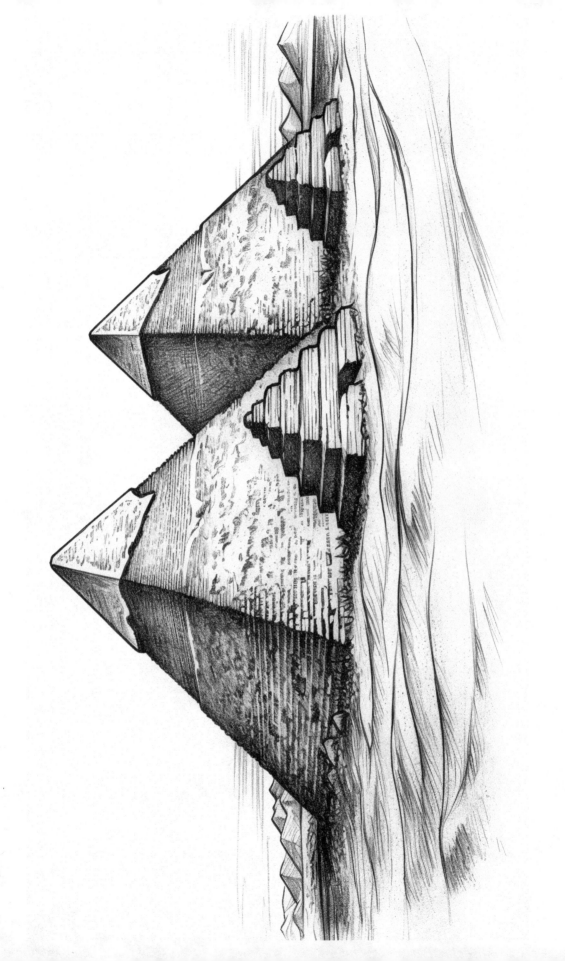

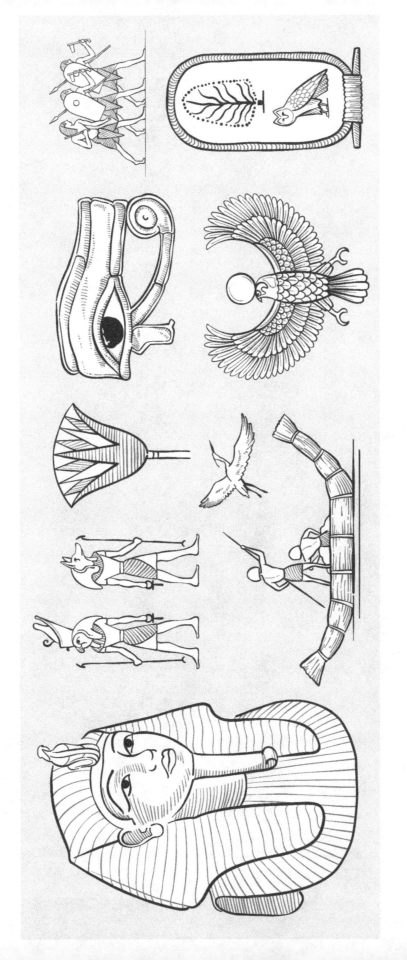

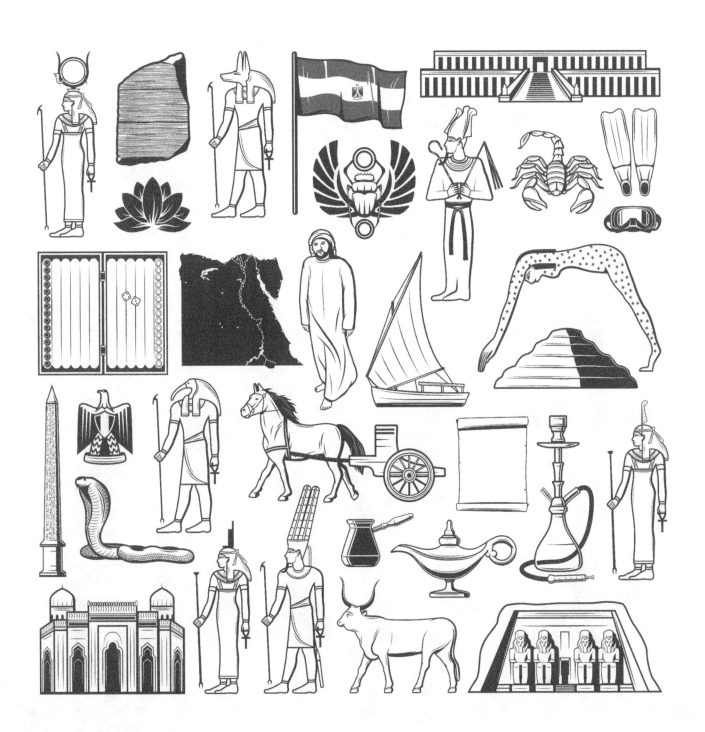

CPSIA information can be obtained
at www.ICGtesting.com
Printed in the USA
BVHW021435130623
665881BV00010B/251